Belong

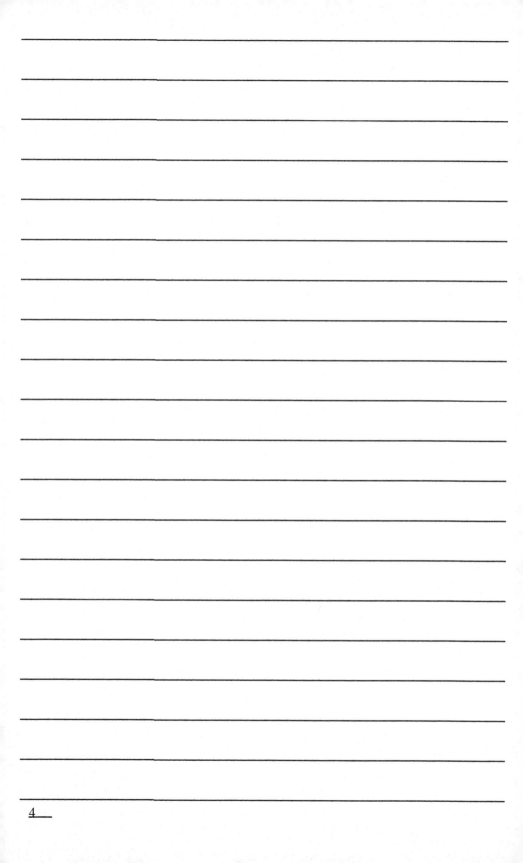

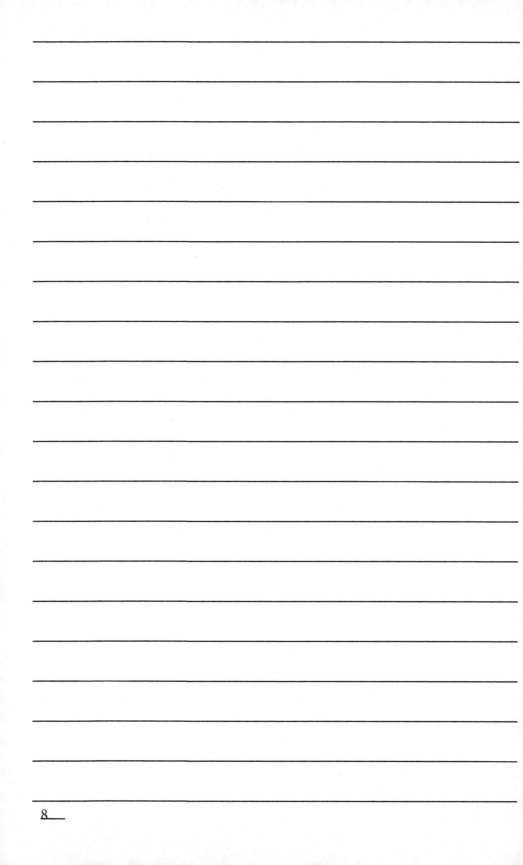

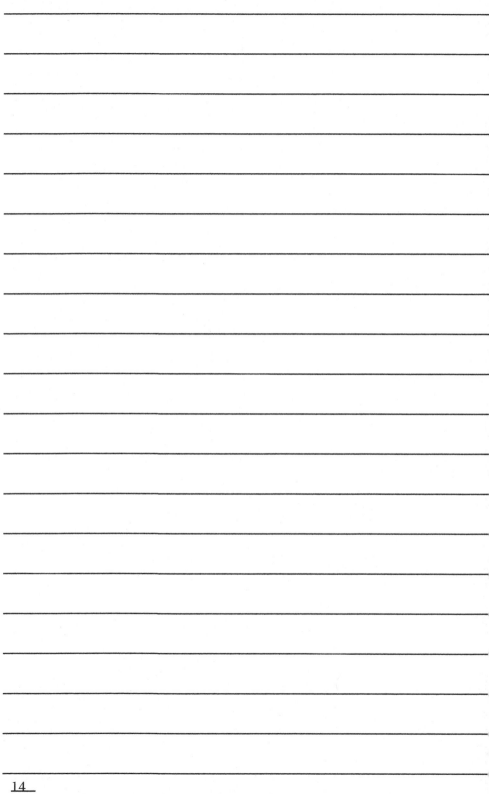

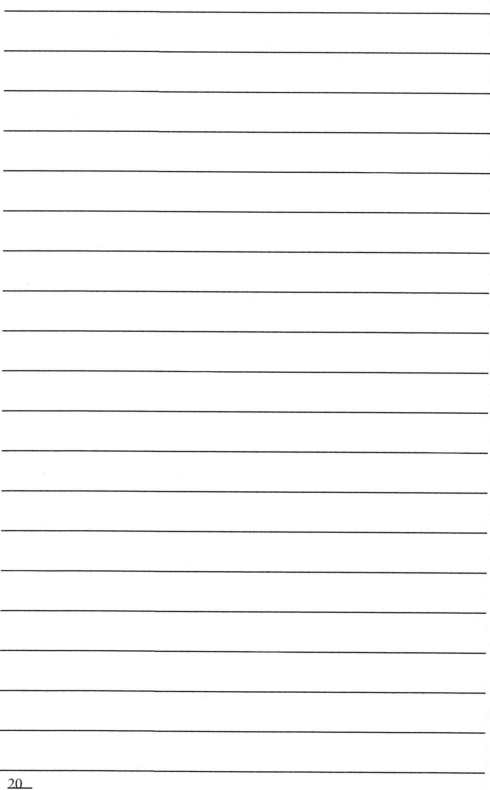

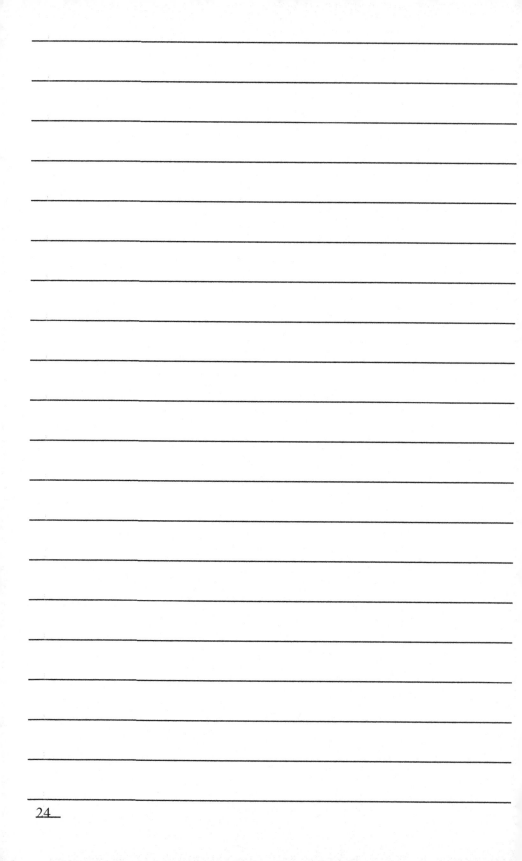

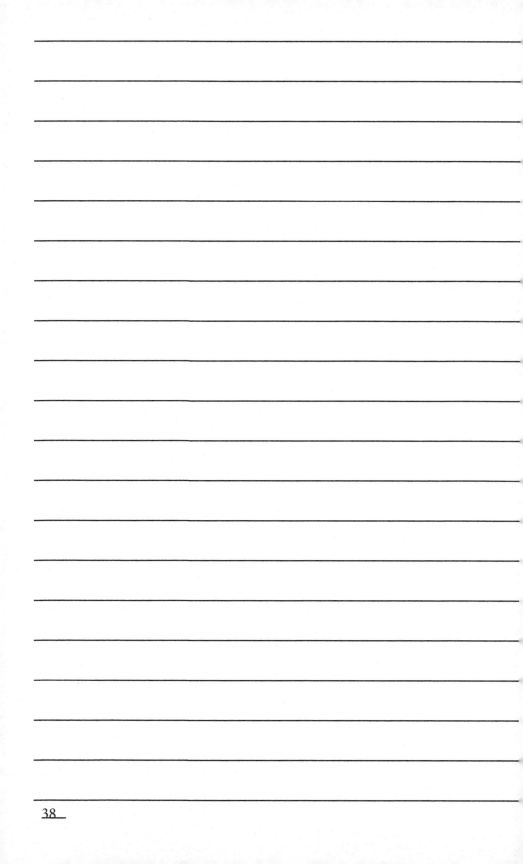

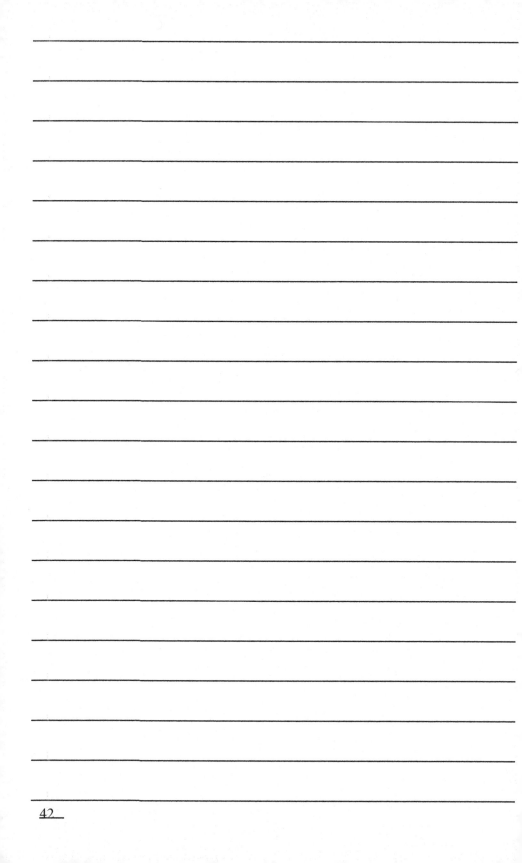

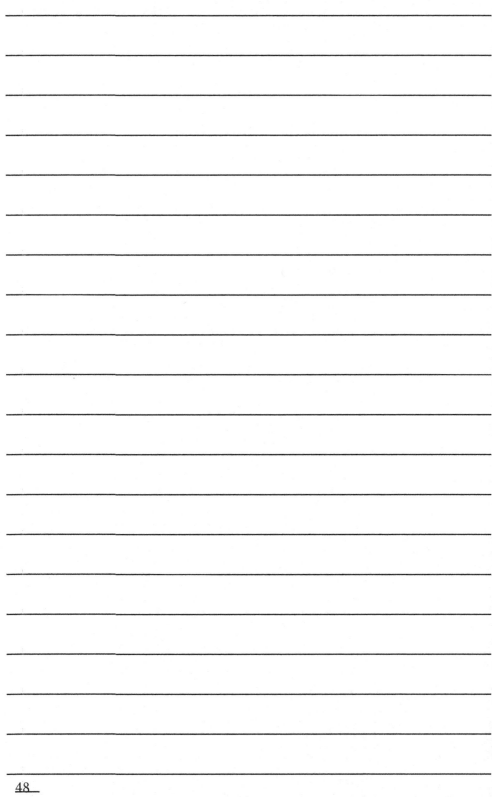

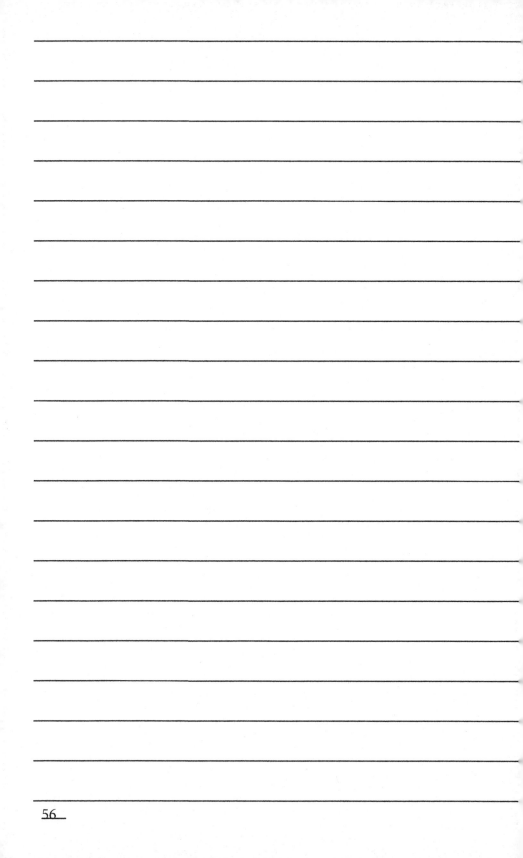

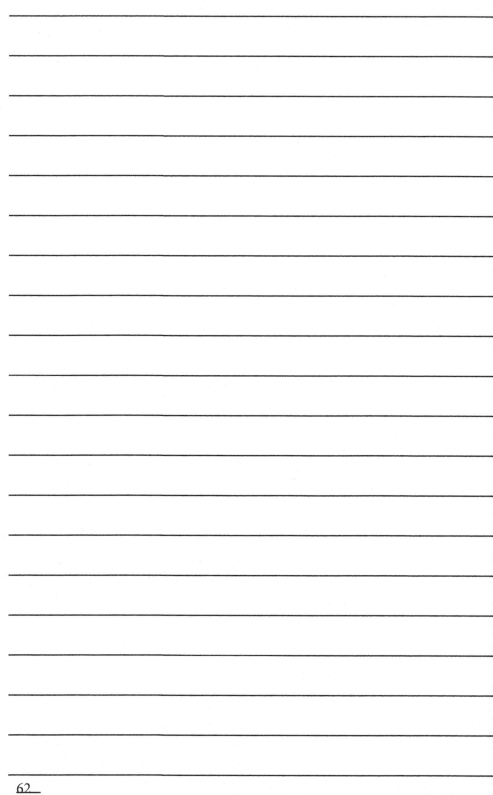

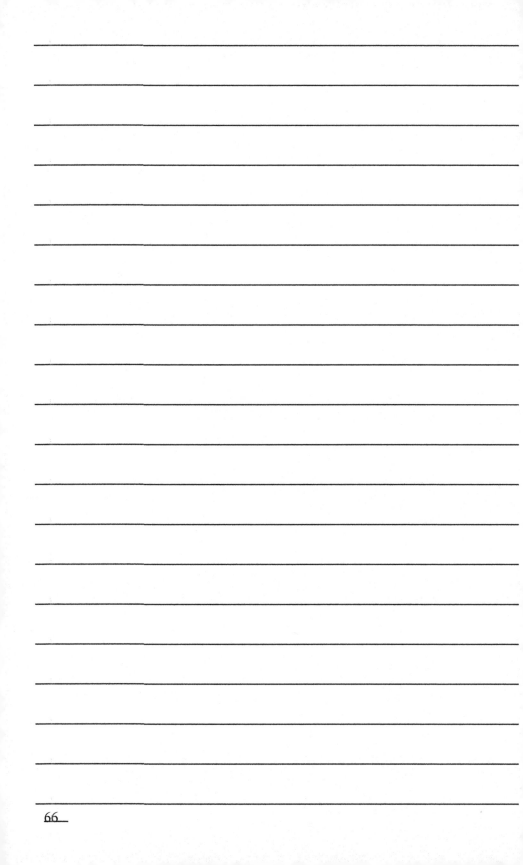

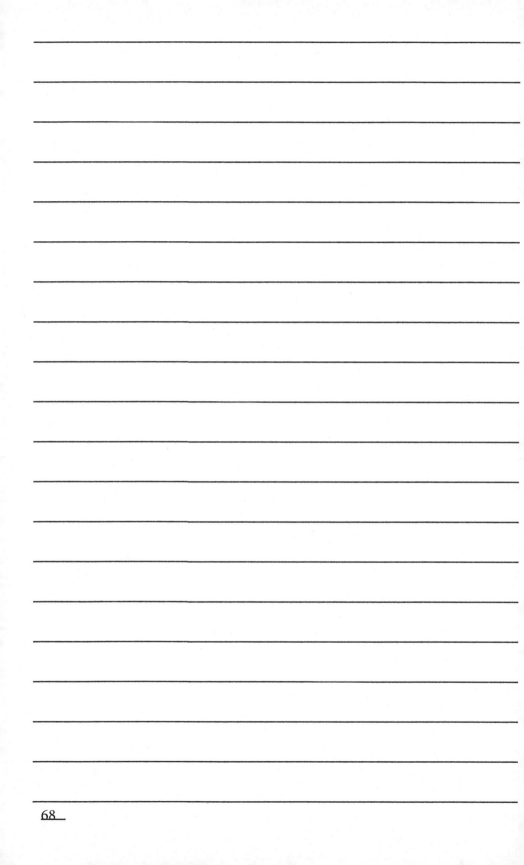

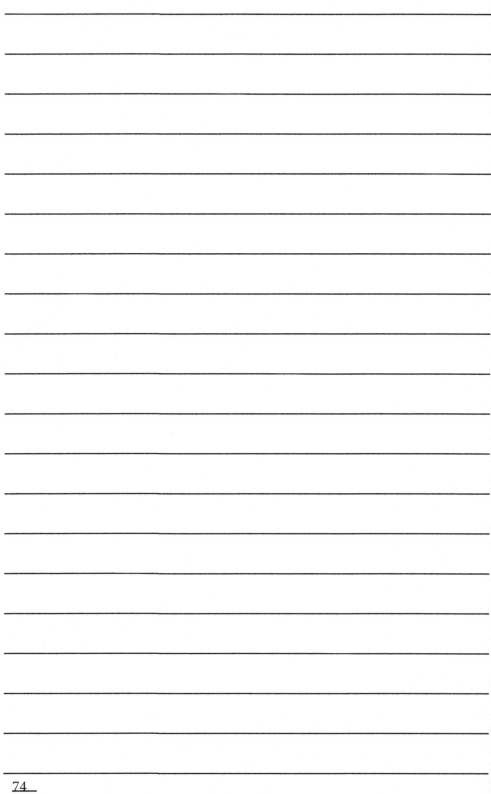

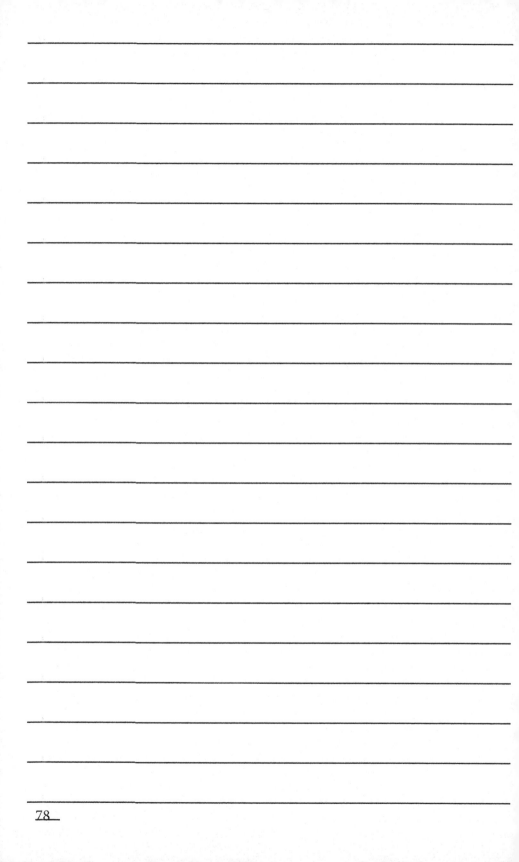

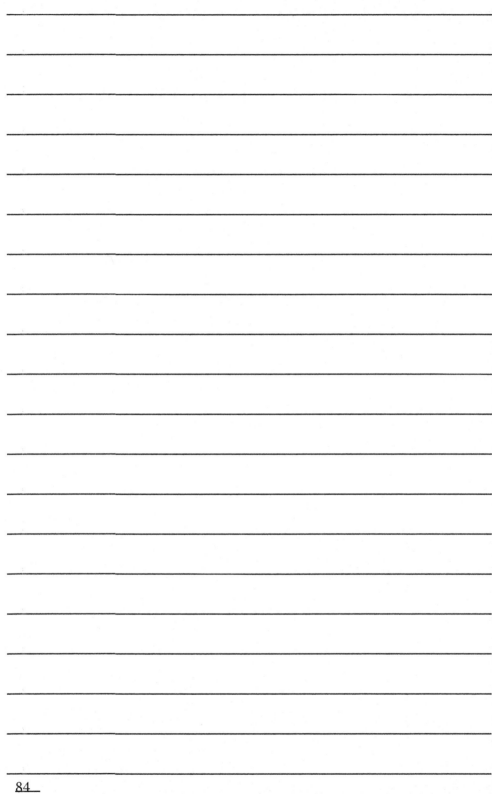

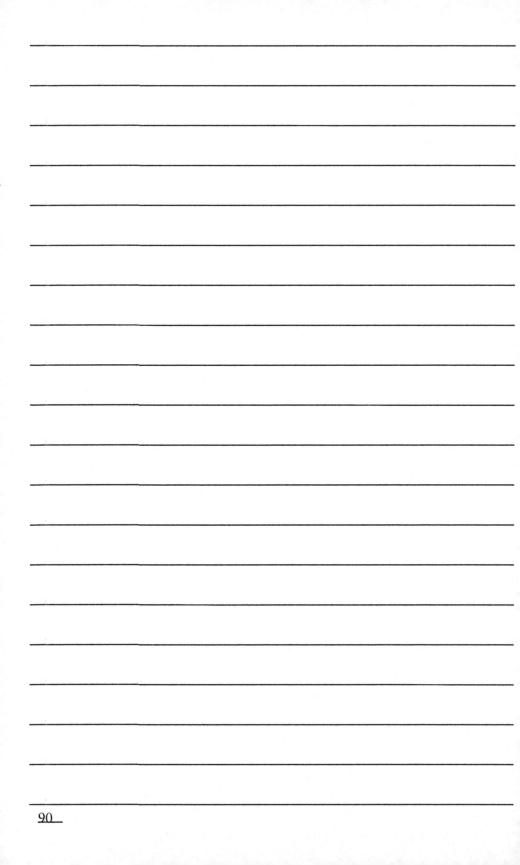

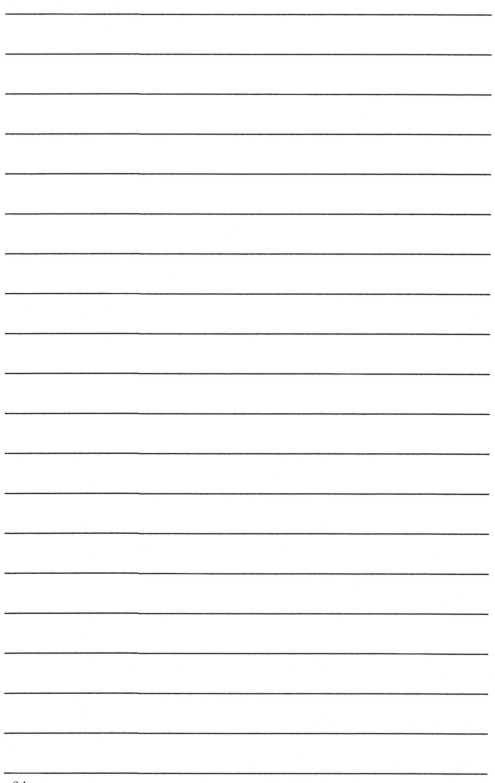

Made in the USA
Monee, IL
01 April 2022

93939129R00056